The Class that Can AT HOME
Coronavirus

written by Riya Jain and JJ Vulopas - illustrated by Bill Dussinger

with your questions answered by Dr. Ruchi Gupta and Dr. Kenneth L. Fox, Jr.

Foreword by Dr. Wendy Sue Swanson

Lancaster, PA

Written by JJ Vulopas & Riya Jain
Illustrations by Bill Dussinger

Printed in the United States of America

ISBN: 978-0-9993845-8-9

For information:
717-205-3856
info@citizensofcan.com
www.citizensofcan.com, www.thelandofcan.com

Citizens Of Can, LLC
1060 Manheim Pike
Lancaster PA 17601

Foreword

Hi, Everybody! I'm so glad you're reading this book, and I'm so glad you're a part of a class that can. To me, as a mom and as a doctor, I can see the incredible value of what you're doing all on your own, in a way I've never seen before. It's amazing how what we do today can change... everything. Our role as just one child or just one adult has the power to change the safety of those everywhere, all over the world. This truth has come into a bright, new focus.

What you do in Minnesota or Tennessee or Washington or Illinois or New York today has an effect on children and their families living everywhere else. All over the planet. Staying home and washing hands and covering your sneezes will help protect children, their families, and their grandparents, all the way over in Australia and India and Iceland and Uganda. YOU-ganda? Yes!!! What YOU do now matters in the most magical way here and all the way over there.

Unlike any time before, we're united in our work to take care of each other, stay safe, and stay home. You're a part of this. This new time where we do school at home, stay in and safe with our families, walk in our neighborhoods and talk with our friends on the computer has changed our lives and made it hard, but it's also shown us how important and interdependent we all are.

We really are connected to everything. One of my favorite environmentalists named John Muir once said, "When we try to pick out anything by itself, we find it hitched to everything else in the Universe." Mr. Muir was right – his work to protect nature in an effort to protect the entire universe couldn't be more true. Your work to protect your own class and home now is just the same.

You're essential and special. We all depend on and celebrate you. Everything you're doing and learning about coronavirus to be a helpful part of our beautiful community will be something you'll know forever. Science is amazing, and this book will help you understand even more about the science of coronavirus and ways to protect yourself, your friends, your teachers, and your family. You get to be a part of something powerful and important. Yes, you can! Here's to you and here's to a safe, happy, connected, and healthy world.

~Dr. Wendy Sue Swanson

Dr. Wendy Sue Swanson is a pediatrician, author and mom. She has devoted her career to prevention efforts and is a spokesperson for the American Academy of Pediatrics. She believes in the value of eating healthy foods, using vaccines to prevent disease, staying home when you're sick and the true value of a good night's sleep. She works to bridge the gap between parents and doctors using digital media. As the first physician blogger for a US pediatric hospital, Dr. Swanson helped lead the way for novel use of social and digital media in health-care. Wendy Sue also needs you to know that she loved being a middle school science teacher in California for a couple years before she went to medical school to become a doctor.

We dedicate this book to YOU for staying strong
and to everyone working to help others.

Today is Can Day.

In our classroom, every day is Can Day!

My name is Collin, and I am a kid from the Land of Can!
I know. I do. I am. I can! I CAN write. That's why my teacher,
Mrs. Can, asked me to write this book.

That's my friend Kayla. She CAN draw. Because Kayla can draw so well, Mrs. Can asked her to illustrate our book.

Mrs. Can's 'Class of Can's' kids CAN! *

My friends CAN. That may sound odd, but it's true. There's even a giant, tongue-twisting, lip-lifting, cheek-chuckling sign that hangs on the wall in front of Can Classroom.

* Repeat this phrase five times as fast as you can, each time getting louder and LOUDer and LOUDER!

Mrs. Can CAN teach. She's kind, creative, and caring. So last week, when Mrs. Can reached out to us, we got very, very excited. Very!

You see, we haven't been in school for more than a month. Something called the coronavirus has caused schools everywhere to close. We now have class on the computer.

"Good morning class!" Mrs. Can exclaimed, as we all watched from home on our devices. "I'm incredibly, convincingly and completely excited to see all of your beautiful, smiling faces!"

"I have two spectacularly special guests joining our Can Cam today," Mrs. Can said. "They're going to talk about a topic many of us are wondering about: the coronavirus."

Mrs. Can smiled, and we heard a familiar sound, a sound signaling something spectacular. It was Mrs. Can banging the Booming Bongos. Like always, we all started drumming on our laps.
pattapattapattapattapattapattapatta

Suddenly, two screens appeared.
"Class, give a wonderful welcome to my friends, Dr. Ruchi Gupta & Dr. Ken Fox," Mrs. Can said. "They care about helping kids just like you!"

The class took turns asking Dr. Ruchi and Dr. Ken questions about the coronavirus. I recorded their answers for our book while Kayla created positively perfect pictures and posters.

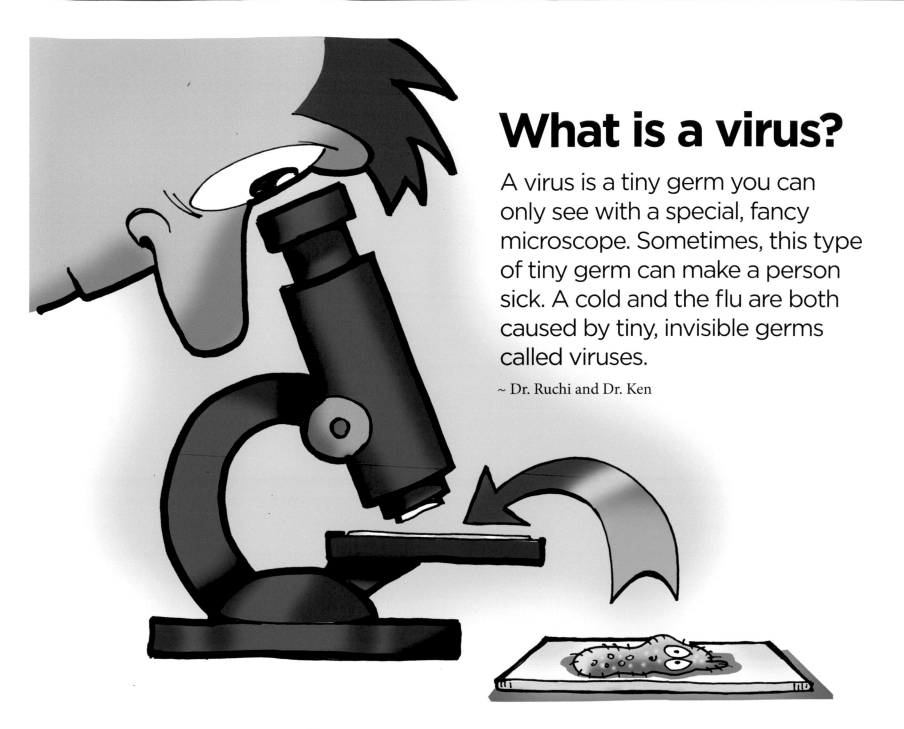

What is a virus?

A virus is a tiny germ you can only see with a special, fancy microscope. Sometimes, this type of tiny germ can make a person sick. A cold and the flu are both caused by tiny, invisible germs called viruses.

~ Dr. Ruchi and Dr. Ken

What is coronavirus?

The coronavirus is a virus that can spread through small wet droplets from the nose or mouth. When a person who has the virus coughs or sneezes, droplets travel through the air up to a distance of about six feet.

In 2019, a new type of coronavirus appeared. Even though the virus is new, we are learning a lot about it. "Corona" means crown. Coronavirus is named for its covering that looks like a crown made of spikes and blobs. Coronavirus is a germ that causes a sickness called COVID-19.

~ Dr. Ruchi and Dr. Ken

Why is this such a big deal?

The coronavirus is a big deal because it can spread easily from person to person. If you catch it, you can get sick.

The good news is when kids get it, they usually don't get very sick from it. However, kids can spread the virus to other kids or other adults.

It is important to know that the coronavirus can make adults and people who have other health problems really sick. The coronavirus has affected people all over the world.

~ Dr. Ruchi and Dr. Ken

Is it okay to feel scared or sad?

It is completely normal to feel scared or sad!

However, many people are looking out for us! Grown ups are here to protect us. They can help us when we feel afraid and when we have questions. Nurses and doctors help sick people feel better. Scientists discover ways to protect and treat everyone. Families and teachers help us learn and take care of us. Neighbors watch out for us.

All the people in our community work together like a shield to keep everyone healthy and safe.

~ Dr. Ruchi and Dr. Ken

16

Why are they closing schools? I miss my friends and teachers.

The most important thing is to stay safe and healthy. We don't want the virus to have the chance to spread from one kid to another.

We have the power to protect ourselves by learning at home instead of at school for now.

One day, we will all be together again. For now, we have to think of all the ways we can stay connected to each other until that day comes.

~ Dr. Ruchi and Dr. Ken

What can I do to be safe?

 You can try to stay indoors as much as possible, but it is ok to go on walks with your family to get fresh air.

 If you do go out, make sure you stay 6 feet apart from people and wash your hands when you come home.

 Wash your hands by rinsing, scrubbing soap for at least 20 seconds, rinsing off the soap, then drying. Make sure to scrub in between fingers, fingernails, fronts, and backs of your hands!

 You can also use hand sanitizer and let it dry for 10 seconds.

 Also, try to sneeze and cough into your elbow or a tissue.

 Doing these things is the best way to stay safe.

~ Dr. Ruchi and Dr. Ken

Will this be forever?

Nope! This virus can't live forever. We are strong, and we will win.

Will we ever go back to normal again?

One day, we will all be together again. We will be able to go to school, see movies, have playdates, play sports, have parties and other celebrations together once again!

Until then, we can use our phones, tablets, computers, pens and paper to stay connected.

~ Dr. Ruchi and Dr. Ken

How do you know we can stop the virus?

We are bigger and stronger and smarter than viruses. ***We will stop the coronavirus!*** Viruses don't have friends. They don't live in neighborhoods. They can't sing or dance. They don't tell stories or jokes.

We laugh. We have hands and we know how to use them: To raise them high; to blow kisses; to wave hello or goodbye; to wipe tears away; to point at something and ask, "What's that?" or "How did that happen?" We can protect ourselves and our communities right now by following the steps to stay safe.

~ Dr. Ruchi and Dr. Ken

20

What are doctors and scientists doing about coronavirus?

Doctors and nurses are working really hard to treat everyone who is sick. Scientists are experimenting to make a vaccine, which is a type of medicine that trains your body to prevent getting sick from the virus.

They are also making better tests to detect the virus and treatments to help you fight the virus. Everyone is doing their part to keep you safe!

~ Dr. Ruchi and Dr. Ken

What can I do to get through this?

We love. No virus can ever take that away. There are so many questions in the world today, but the answer is always love.

We love our families, friends, teachers, nurses, doctors, and communities. We are strong and brave. We work together. We help each other, even if we feel sad, worried, or lost.

Coronavirus may wear a crown, but we have the power. **We rule. Kid power!**

~ Dr. Ruchi and Dr. Ken

What if we want to know more about the coronavirus?

You may have other questions. It is important that your family has the most accurate information available about coronavirus, which is why Mrs. Can and her friends created a special webpage with extra resources and links!

www.citizensofcan.com/coronavirus

As we finished asking our questions, we began to feel better, especially since we knew what we could control to stay healthy. "I'm not so scared anymore," Maya said.

"It's important to ask questions when you don't understand something," Mrs. Can said. "Now let's give a tongue-twisting, lip-lifting, cheek-chuckling 'Thank You' to Dr. Ruchi and Dr. Ken!"

We all waved as Mrs. Can threw her hands into the air and gave us all a special look. We all knew what she was going to say. "Mrs. Can's 'Class of Can's' kids can..." Mrs. Can shouted, pointing to us to finish the sentence.

"...STAY HEALTHY!"

Dr. Kenneth L. Fox, Jr.

Dr. Fox does community pediatrics. He was appointed Chief Health Officer of Chicago Public Schools in December 2016. A Chicago native, Dr. Fox has worked in primary care for over 25 years in Boston, Chicago and Philadelphia – in university and community clinics, hospitals, mission teams, an orphanage, a psychiatric ward and in private practice. He's a graduate of the University of Chicago, trained at Boston Children's Hospital and was an RWJ Clinical Scholar at the University of Pennsylvania. Bridging the disciplines of pediatric primary care and medical anthropology, Dr. Fox has served on medical school faculties—Harvard, Penn, Boston University, Northwestern and the University of Chicago—and held appointments at BU and Harvard School of Public Health. He's worked on a range of editorial and non-profit boards and received grants and fellowships from the Ford, Fulbright, Robert Wood Johnson (RWJ) and Kellogg Foundations, The Open Society Institute on Medicine as a Profession, and the Institute for Health and Social Justice. He's currently an RWJ Foundation Clinical Scholar. He's written and lectured widely on cultural and social justice issues in health and care and collaborated with Partners in Health and Physicians for Human Rights. His longstanding interests in global health have led him to work in Panama, Haiti, the Dominican Republic and South Africa.

Dr. Ruchi Gupta

Dr. Gupta is a Professor of Pediatrics and Medicine at Northwestern Medicine and has more than 16 years of experience as a board-certified pediatrician and health researcher. Dr. Gupta completed her undergraduate and medical education at the University of Louisville, and continued on to complete her medical residency at Children's Hospital & Regional Medical Center, University of Washington in Seattle, WA. She completed her pediatric health services research fellowship at Boston Children's Hospital and Harvard Medical School, and went on to receive her Masters of Public Health from the Harvard School of Public Health. Dr. Gupta is the director of the Center for Food Allergy & Asthma Research (CFAAR) within Northwestern's Institute for Public Health and Medicine (IPHAM) and is a clinical attending at Ann & Robert H. Lurie Children's Hospital Chicago, where she is involved in clinical, epidemiological, and community-based research. She is internationally recognized for her groundbreaking research in childhood food allergy and asthma prevalence. She has also significantly contributed to academic research surrounding economic costs, pediatric management, ED visits and hospitalizations, quality of life and community interventions, especially in schools. An author of *The Food Allergy Experience*, Dr. Gupta has over 100 publications and her work has been featured in major TV networks and print media.

Riya Jain

Riya Jain is an 8th grader in Chicago, IL. She co-authored *The Class That Can: Food Allergies* and all the books in *The Class That Can: Staying Healthy* series. She has been in multiple videos educating young people on health issues.

She is a student advocate, President of Student Council, and loves school - even if it is at home right now! She enjoys playing tennis, basketball, and piano.

Riya believes in developing a "CAN mindset" so you can focus on the positive and all the amazing things you CAN do!!

Bill Dussinger

Bill is an award-winning graphic designer, illustrator and educator from Lititz, PA. He has a BS degree in Art Education from Kutztown University. Bill has been in the design business for over 30 years for many clients such as Discovery Channel, the Oakland Raiders, East Coast Music Hall of Fame and Hershey Entertainment and Resorts. He currently teaches graphic design and illustration at Pennsylvania College of Art & Design in Lancaster, PA. In his spare time he loves to visit his four grandchildren, paint watercolor paintings and watch college football.
Penny Lane Graphics, www.plgraphics.com

Jamison "JJ" Vulopas

With an approach that educators have called transformational, JJ inspires young people everywhere to become "Citizens of Can" by embracing the 14 Words of Can. His youth-empowerment resources are used by schools and pediatricians' offices nationwide. JJ is the author of *Land of Not*, *The Class That Can: Food Allergies*, and *The Class That Can: Staying Healthy* series. An analyst at Lucid Management and Capital Partners LP, JJ is a 2019 graduate of the Wharton School of the University of Pennsylvania. He lives in New York City.

Mrs. Can

Mrs. Can CAN teach! Mrs. Can is the ultimate teacher, the one who inspires and empowers and compels every one of her students to be the best versions of themselves. In Mrs. Can's class, every child is accepted, appreciated, acknowledged and cared for. Not just for one day. Every day.

By introducing her students to the 14 Words of Can, and by following the tenets outlined in the Can Constitution, Mrs. Can knows that she is creating a classroom of life-long leaders, a classroom where students will define themselves by their cans, look out for each other, and, ultimately, soar!

The Book that Started the whole CAN CRAZE!

A SMART book with a POWERFUL message!

When 9-year-old Collin (Yep, the same Collin from this book) moves with his family from the Land of Can to the Land of Not, he is shocked to discover that everyone in his new school is sad. With the help of his parents, Collin devises a plan to show his new friends that happiness comes from embracing who they are and who they can be, not who they're not.

As a veteran educator said, "JJ's *Land of Not* will inspire, empower and transform all children to understand thier possibilities rather than define themselves by their limitations."

NOT THE ILLUSTRATOR: J.J. VULOPAS   NOT THE AUTHOR: BILL DUSSINGER

Visit www.citizensofcan.com

Do your children know the 13* words of CAN?

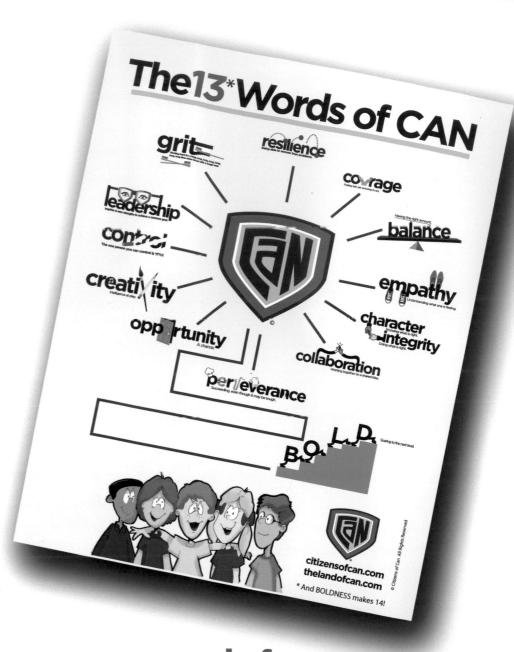

The 13* Words of CAN

grit · resilience · courage · leadership · balance · control · creativity · empathy · opportunity · character integrity · collaboration · perseverance · BOLD

citizensofcan.com
thelandofcan.com

* And BOLDNESS makes 14!

Mrs. Can's students do!

We have amazing resources ready for you.
Visit www.citizensofcan.com

* And BOLDNESS makes 14!

THANK YOU, TEACHERS AND EDUCATORS, FOR ALL THAT YOU DO!
From the Center for Food Allergy and Asthma (CFAAR) and the Center for Community Health (CCH).

TEACHING IS A WORK OF HEART!

CFAAR is a part of the Institute for Public Health and Medicine (IPHAM) at Northwestern University's Feinberg School of Medicine and Ann & Robert H Lurie Children's Hospital of Chicago. CCH is a part of IPHAM.